Someday, Somewhere

Someday, Somewhere

Photographs and Poems

DAVID JENNINGS

RESOURCE *Publications* · Eugene, Oregon

SOMEDAY, SOMEWHERE
Photographs and Poems

Resource Publications
An Imprint of Wipf and Stock Publishers
199 W. 8th Ave., Suite 3
Eugene, OR 97401

www.wipfandstock.com

PAPERBACK ISBN: 978-1-6667-8424-4
HARDCOVER ISBN: 978-1-6667-8425-1
EBOOK ISBN: 978-1-6667-8426-8

VERSION NUMBER 07/31/23

To my wife, Kristin: Thank you for the love, time, space, and support needed to follow my passions of photography and writing. I love you.

To my daughter, Reagan: Thank you for being my photography buddy on so many outings, often impromptu and in pursuit of sunsets! I have loved every minute. Maybe a sunset or two, when you are old, will *take you back years, years ago*. . . Trust God in all things and believe in yourself. I love you.

To my dad: Thank you for instilling in me the appreciation you always showed for the little things. I see all life as precious because of you, and give grace to any home-invading creatures by way of cup and tissue because of your example. I never see geese fly over without thinking of you. I love and miss you.

To my mom: Thank you for a lifetime of your love, laughter and favor. In your passing, the miracle of death became as evident to me as is the miracle of birth. I understand why you were in such a hurry to 'go home.' You are home, now—with Dad and Mark and baby Robert. I love and miss you so much.

Set a frame where you can see
Beyond the shape of house and tree
An hour or so before the day
Is set to slowly fade away
Then watch the artist brush and blend
A work too great to comprehend.

First will fall a few fine flakes—
There. And there. And there.
Like a dandelion makes
In a breath of air.

Then, as when a shaker shakes,
Snow flies everywhere.
Ecstatic—dazed—a child awakes
From sleeping, unaware.

What is it from me that you need?
Why is it that you stare?
It seems each time I come for seed,
I find you looking there:
Your fingers pulling back the shade—
You pointing at the glass,
As if I earn some accolade
For pecking at your grass.

It isn't that I mind, per se.
It's just, I want to know:
Why is it, when I fly away,
It leaves you looking so?

Feathered tremblings, peck and scratch.
Were that I could light a match
And get you near and keep you warm
Until this bitter, blowing storm
Runs its course—or better yet
Were that I could somehow let
All of you—each tiny thing,
Shielded by exhausted wing—
Come inside and make a choir
Chirp by chirp beside my fire.

Something's going on inside,
They've pulled the shade down low.
I think that old man might have died.
I'll have to look to know.

Mother cannot see me there,
She'd have me by my neck!
But this far back and with that glare,
I've got to go and check.

His eyes look closed, but maybe one
Is open—I can't tell.
His ribs are still. His shirt's undone.
His face is thin and pale.

I'm scared they'll see me looking in!
They've moved him from his bed
Onto a cart—strange mannequin.
I'm pretty sure he's dead.

Let's have ours be the first steps that have crossed
Since this snow fell. Let's forge the woodland trail
  As if our own and risk becoming lost!
  Let's feign a fame immortal if we fail.

  And all the creatures that we find we'll claim:
No bird nor squirrel nor owl has yet been learned.
  Let's play the world is ours to note and name
  And leave no distant, hidden rock unturned!

   Let's go as far as daylight will allow
  Then set ourselves on somehow getting back:
Where each path splits, we'll pause and furrow brow
   Before we share relief at finding track.

   Let's forge the woodland trail as if our own
   And flag this day to find when you are grown.

I drag myself across the sky
With rarely but a glimpse from you.
I cycle through from full to new
And back—yet you don't bat an eye.

I change the tides to low and high.
You think it's something they just do.
This is no phase I'm going through.
They call me blue—you wonder why.

But then—as if I were to die—
This morning, sinking from your view,
You rushed around as I withdrew
To photograph my rote goodbye.

Tonight I'll pass like déjà vu:
No glance. No look. No ahh. No ooh.

I thought I'd be the first one there
To see the sunrise come.
The fields were full already, though,
In stridulating hum.
A mockingbird sang unashamed
Until my step made need
To stop, move one fence-length down,
Grab wire and then proceed.
Below, along the riverbank,
One hundred toads swapped croaks
Like chatter—imperceptible—
Of animated folks.
All this and then it was as if
Creation drew breath in
And turned to the horizon, stunned,
To see the sun again!

I've made a circled path around
The post you've chained me to:
A scar from pacing over ground
With nothing else to do.

I used to hope for going in,
Oh—thrill when I was small!
My heart would race for you, back then—
My ears would beg your call.

But days, then weeks, then months—now years—
Have worn away my soul:
Left out—restrained—life disappears.
Hope dies chained to a pole.

My world is outlined by the trace
Of dirt—the scar—I've made:
I sleep to dream a different place
And wake to try for shade.

I'd guess you don't know where you're going.
This is your third time by.
No one—if they're right in knowing—
Comes way out here, so why
Would it be you keep on passing
By on my dirt road?
I'd call you out for cow harassing
But I feel you're owed
The likelihood that being lost
Is why you're trailing dust.
Forgive the way my tail is tossed—
I have a thing with trust.

Little one, below your nest:
Tiny frame and naked chest—
Separated from the rest.
Kicked out. Denied. Dispossessed.

Helpless in your only flight—
Downed to earth from such a height.
Take my daughter's whispered rite
To your garden grave tonight.

Gone before your hum is heard,
Feeder—flower—feeder—twig.
Bullet-like, your motion blurred,
Save for when you steal a swig
From provision we have hung
Or from lilac chaste tree blooms,
Trapping nectar on your tongue—
Suspended—then your flight resumes.

Feeder—twig—flower—drawn
To the neighbor's garden—gone!

So many times, no map, no plan,
The open road would call
And I would set off with my man—
Air thick with aerosol
That held that other girl's hair still
Against the reckless wind—
To shred the backroads, dressed to kill
And rowdy, to offend.

For years we ran the countryside
Then something strange took place:
That other girl grew out and wide
And he shut down my pace
To nothing but a cautious crawl—
So slow, each time we went,
I feared that I would gasp and stall
And die of discontent.

Then one last time—*Not yet! Not yet!*—
My pedal pressed the floor.
That other girl stretched out in sweat,
Her feet pressed to my door.
We screeched through lights and spit out dust
And jumped a curb to stop.
With grunts and groans she gasped and cussed—
Lord! It's about to drop!

So many times, no tires, no gas,
I've fantasized that feel
Of grinding gravel to harass—
His hands gripped to my wheel!
Years, years have gone—the baby, grown.
That other girl has died.
He comes out seldom—skin and bone—
And looks, then goes inside.

I've got a photograph that shows
A father sharing what he knows
Of depth of field and shadow-light
And rule of thirds to left or right
And how the gifts of God appear
In cosmos far and flower near
And in the minutes—one by one—
Spent between a father-son.

He'd spent so many years at sea
His feet still stumbled clumsily
On land, as if, incessantly,
The waves were churning still.

His arms would flail to tell the thrill
Of beast and serpent he would kill
As bottled port would slosh and spill
Like splashes from a swell.

Oh, the stories he would tell!
Floundering until he fell
Again into the holding cell
To let his liquor clear.

One hand would feign to hold a *bring 'em near*—
The other gripped the bars as if to steer.

I'd thought to stop a thousand times before.
I'd even pressed my knuckles to your door
About to knock, then turned and walked away.
What if you did not know me anymore?

Or worse, what if you did—what would you say?
I'd left so smug, yet in such disarray,
I wasn't sure we'd ever talk again.
I should have known that it would go this way:

Of course you'd grab my arm and pull me in
As if the things I'd done had never been—
As if no bridge I'd crossed had ever burned—
As if you'd known I would be back, and when.

Your love—your grace—was never lost or earned.
I should have known your lock was never turned.

I've seen the remnants—blood and shell—
That marked the times you've tried,
For reasons only you could tell,
To reach the other side
Of highways rumbling ever-crammed
With traffic—no delay—
Such that any chance was damned
To end in crushed display.

I stop and carry you across
When circumstances grant.
Oh! Heavy weighs that albatross
I wear those times I can't.
It's then I pray God seizes you
And turns you in your track,
And why I fix a forward view
Afraid of looking back.

Before the sun slips through the trees I hear
The birds announcing that they are awake,
Not long before the highest branches shake
And squirrels in chase show tail then disappear.

I listen, sipping coffee in my swing,
As varied voices—chirped and whistled calls—
Fly out from where the drooping fence vine sprawls:
Exultant, frenzied, feathered worshipping!

I fill their feeders full of fruit and seed
And overflow the squirrel box with cracked corn
(As I did yesterday, I would have sworn!)
Then watch all those descend that had been treed.

In song they thank me from their tray and bowl—
Or is that singing coming from my soul?

He'd seen himself led out into the yard:
Tripping, struggling—dragged beside the guard.
He'd seen his own feet stumble on the stairs.
He'd seen those other two bound in their snares—
Black bags over their heads tied off with rope.
He'd felt the noose choke out his breath and hope.
He'd heard the hush spread through the crowd as all
Waited for the wink to make them fall.
He'd heard the crack as trap doors opened wide.
He'd seen his body swinging when he died.
He'd heard the gasps and shrieks and chatter grow
As each rope loosed and let the bodies go.

He'd died a hundred deaths before the day
The guard and priest—eyes down—led him away.

I've checked the pasture horses from the fence.
They like to watch me when I clean my paws
But will not have me near them ever since
That time I scratched one of them with my claws.
I've walked the porch three times. Still, no one's there
And nothing has been added to my plate
Since earlier today. I've jumped from chair
To windowsill to make them watch me wait
With no success. I've searched the barn for pests
And chased a mouse to hide under the hay
Which made the swallows scatter from their nests
And brought the donkey breathless with his bray.

Now that I've had a moment for myself,
I think I'll go and push things off a shelf.

Find us in your flight among
Our field of flowering plants.
Take my nectar with your tongue
And fill your furry pants
Full of pollen you can drop
Like little fertile freight
On my neighbor when you stop
And help us pollinate.

I've leaned so long my elbows ache,
My fingers have gone numb—
Not sure of if I sleep or wake
Or dusk or dawn has come.

I hear the ticking of the clock,
It lulls me into trance:
Cornered in my own cellblock,
Crushed by this huge expanse.

I've wondered how true inmates deal
With four cold walls and time.
At least one day I can appeal—
Remembrance is no crime.

Each breath I breathe, I fog the glass.
I've nothing else to do
But start—each time a car goes past—
To think it could be you.

Under God, this favored nation.
Less so, it seems, each generation.
From home, from school the slow negation
Of what was once our fixed foundation
Cancelled by a flawed filtration
Focused on contrite placation—
Twisted truths through loose translation
Such that now with hesitation
Is any credit for Creation
Granted God but in citation,
Subject yet to cancellation
And perhaps the allocation
Of some proper compensation
If it causes violation
Of any person's affirmation
Or makes them tense in conversation.
Any hope for conservation
Of this rare and favored nation
Rests on heads held in prostration
Rueful for our profanation.

I tried to catch a wave today
In my little net.
Each one crashed in and slipped away.
I've caught nothing yet
Except some strands of seaweed and
Bits of broken shell
I'll take instead, along with sand,
For my show and tell.

You could hear the band from blocks away—
Blaring brass broke through the heat of day
As bass and snare drums made bystanders sway
With every beat of every song they'd play.

The horse that pulled the hearse that held the dead
Strolled steadily behind the man who led
The proud procession ploddingly ahead—
Its clip-clop echoed each step it would tread.

No one in parade appeared distraught.
If any tears were witnessed, they were not
Of sadness but of joy! The box was brought
With bliss unbridled to the graveyard plot.

Only there did all the noise fall still,
Save for the widow's wailing—awful, shrill.

Somehow seed achieves its spot
And anchors down with prodding root
Then gasps for air with rising shoot
And shows its feelers overwrought
With leaves that turn the light to starch
And give the sapling strength to grow.
All this a hundred years ago
For each great trunk and knotted arch
That towers over tiny me.
Don't tell me what I cannot be!

I knew not where the rest had gone
Nor what had happened to the boat
   Nor what it was I held fast to.
      I was alive was all I knew:
    Alone. Afraid. Awash. Afloat.
A fleck the fish would feed upon.

Above, the clouds would boil and churn
And flash and crack and groan and hiss
   As wave on wave swept over me.

Below was nothing but the sea.
   I was a speck for the abyss
   To toss about and overturn.

How it was that I was found
I knew not—nor where I awoke
Nor whom I owed my life in debt.
   I was alive—no longer wet.
  No longer frantic not to choke
Nor flailing feet to find the ground.

I was alive was all I knew.
But where—in that dark deep—were you?

27

It's true the fields go on forever here.
No, nothing pains me when I run the skies.
Never have I splashed through streams so clear,
Nor heard such howling chorus harmonize.

I've yet to dig and lack for finding bone.
And scents—almost too many to take in!
This pure elation I have never known,
Save when you spoke and scratched under my chin.

He said the streets were slick with rain
And full of faces wrenched with pain
Or yelling out in shrill disdain:
How cruel! How mean! How inhumane!
He said he'd stamped a bloody stain
On every brick of every lane,
Breaking bone and bruising brain
Before the fallen could regain
The strength to try and run again.
He said he'd been somewhere in Spain,
Then gave the grass another pull.

I think it was a bunch of bull.

Remind me of the selfless brave
Who gave their blood and breath.
Let me hear, each time you wave,
    Their rally cries in death.
Tell me of the times they fought
When bomb blasts broke the night:
Courageous, although cornered, caught—
    Their desperate, daring fight.
Whisper, when you're borne by wind,
    The prayers that you have heard

Pleading that the pain would end—
    Garbled. Injured, Slurred.
Show me proven acts of pride
    In body-tarnished sands.
Give me grasp of grief defied
    By bloodied, lifeless hands.
Raise my chest and thrill my heart
    Each time I see you fly:
This great nation, set apart,
    Esteem and glorify!

Grow me as a sunflower grows.
Teach me what its life force knows.
Face me east to greet the sun.
Turn me as its track is run.
Keep my face toward the light.
My petals—heat! My soul—ignite!
Droop me as the night comes on.
Turn me east to seek the dawn.

Losing three to five with two men on.
Two outs and all but one last inning gone.
The pitcher cleared the rubber free of dirt,
Smearing spit-wet fingers on his shirt
While checking runners with a sideways glance
As ball and glove combined in pitching stance.

This—this was what he'd dreamed of every day
Of his young life. This was the play-by-play
That he'd announced through makeshift megaphone
To every willing friend he'd ever known
So many times that they would call it too.
What happened next, his mind already knew:

He pointed high above the outfield wall
And knocked the cover clean off of that ball.

You couldn't call his squeaks and chatter song.
No—it was nothing you could whistle to
Nor did it haunt from something you once knew
Nor did it beg for you to sing along.

It seemed to be erratically composed
Like eager talk between two mice at play
With rising pitch the more they had to say,
Or angry talk between two mice opposed.

But he filled that graveyard with his sound
As if he'd been commissioned by the dead
To soak the soil with singing overhead
From branch then fence then stone then grassy mound.

That his song was only squeaks and chatter
To me, and all the dead, did not matter.

I wait even until the last
Most distant rumble goes,

Until the final flash has passed
And trailing wind gust blows

Before I leave the cellar light
And start to climb the stair—

Afraid of finding out what might
No longer be found there.

It's strange how loud a hinge can be
With no one coming in.
The lack of creaking wide and shut
Time and time again
With glad hellos and slow goodbyes—
How it once had been—
Screeches through my ears all day
Gnawing my nerves thin
And leaves me longing with my hands
Holding up my chin.

Do you think my years are showing?
It seems my go is slowly slowing
And this shell I'm always towing
Whorl on whorl on whorl keeps growing.

Anything I do takes time:
Each inch I move I have to slime
Then heave myself through grit and grime.
And God forbid I have to climb!

I don't know how much more I've got.
In fact, I've lately had the thought
Of laying claim to some safe spot
Perhaps inside a flowerpot

Where I could rest and count the days
Until my shell and I part ways.

That moment—Oh! That instant
When life and death combine,
That last brief breath, but remnant,
Where is and was define.
What secrets in that second—split—
When last the heart has thrust!
Time stays though the clock has quit.
We pray. We doubt. We trust.
Oh! To stand where you have stood
With one hand on the gate,
To leave this all behind for good
And know—not speculate!

Stripped of clothes and robed in scorn.
Crowned in twisted, tangled thorn.
Nailed and hanged and left to die:
Son of God. King. Adonai.

Quaking earth and darkened sun.
Forgive. Forsaken? It is done.
Taken to the grave and kept.
Risen as the mourners wept.

Linens folded, stone withdrawn:
Tell the others he is gone!

I see them point my way and stare,
Just look at that poor cat!
As if they've found—in baited snare—
Some barely breathing rat.

I hear them talk about my eye
And purr with confidence
To know the tattered reason why
They have not seen you since.

This shrinking pond will have to do.
It's wet, at least for now,
And big enough for one or two
Overheating cow.

But if the herd has heard the word
About our small retreat,
There soon will be—for a tiny bird—
No room to dip its feet.

They've put away his tractor keys
And taken all his guns.
You'll no more have the use for these.
His car no longer runs.

A lady cleans his house and clothes
And helps to keep him fed.
You're old now—that's the way this goes.
He can't hear what she's said.

On warm days he sits in the chair
That looks out on his land.
What are you seeing when you stare?
He rubs his calloused hand.

At night he smells the burning oil
And feels the plow drag deep.
Put me out there in that soil.
He prays to die or sleep.

Before they ever came to blows
Their rumbled growls and screaming rose
The way that talk and taunting grows
    With fighters in the ring.

Antlers gouged at grass to sling
As two bull elk were circling,
Each wondering who would start the thing
    And then the rivals clashed.

Head-to-head the great beasts crashed—
Racks interlocked and tugged and thrashed
In show of manhood, unabashed,
    To win the estrus cow.

No victor would the fray allow—
She wasn't watching anyhow.

You will never know how hard I tried
To crown you with this wreath before you died.
I grabbed what blooms and buds the yard supplied
And started weaving (some I left untied!)
The moment that I heard that you were ill.

They must have thought me mad. I was wild-eyed
And gasping breath from there to here, full stride—
Sobbing all the while, undignified,
Only to find the doctor by your side
Telling me you weren't, and never will.

How many times I hinted or implied
But never said it out—and I do still!

You left the life you said you loved:
What kind of person leaves
A pregnant wife and crying child
Pulling at her sleeves?
Who tears apart their mother's heart
In trade for some strange shore,
Swearing that you'd see her soon
While staring at the floor?
Your father, since the day you went,
Was stripped of any rest,
Awake each night—in fear for you—
Hands gripped against his chest.
You left the land you said you loved.
Thank God for those like you
Who give up all to keep us free—
The brave, the proud, the few.

I still can feel my dad's hands holding me—
Half lifted up, half balanced on his knee:
Now look right here and tell me what you see.
One quarter brought my wildest whims in view.

I see a jungle. Maybe it's a zoo?
A bear. A lion. There's a kangaroo.
The trees are full of monkeys swinging through.
I think I see the ocean—there's the shore!

He would grin and let my eye explore
Whatever sights my mind was searching for
Until it wasn't working anymore
And he would put another quarter in.

I wish life were the way it was back then:
One coin and I could briefly dream again.

I wish they hadn't moved me here.
I've made no new friends since
That day—whatever was the year—
I took this residence.

The others up and down this street
Seem quite content to stay
Locked in—forgotten, obsolete—
In leisurely decay.

No, I'm not one to lie around—
I don't fit in here well.
It's just, so far, I haven't found
A soul whom I can tell.

You've slipped the line that held you here
And drifted off to sea.
I watched you float and disappear,
Knotted helplessly.

I hope the strange, far-off allure
That made you tug and heave
Is worth the parting from my moor
And ruin of my weave.

I thought, at first, to close the gate
That someone had left wide
For fear of letting out the souls
Supposed to stay inside.

But if they'd had the aim to leave
They could have gone long since:
Only living things are bound
By a boneyard fence.

Waves would chase the birds up hill—
The birds would chase them back
As they returned once more to fill
The sea's next soaked attack.

As if they were two kids at play—
Tag, you're it! Now you!
One would rush—one run away:
Be prey, and then pursue.

Back and forth the game recurred
Amid resounding swish,
And then I saw the winning bird
Bring up a tiny fish.

Somehow our wires have gotten crossed—
Our most important lessons lost.
What love for God or neighbor? Self?
And all at such an awful cost.

With no foundation, what can stand?
Yet build and build and build on sand.
Then comes the rain and flood and fall
And we cry, stubborn, *what command?*

We punish prayer, shame God, praise sin
And wonder why a man walks in
And bang bang bang bang bang bang bang
Then puts the gun up to his chin.

Somehow our wires have gotten crossed—
And all at such an awful cost.

What was it like to reawaken,
Two days old when you were taken—
Held against an angel's chest?
Did you think she was your mother,
Having never known another,
When she sighed and softly pressed
Her lips against your little head—
When she patted you and said
Sweet dreams and laid you down to rest?

I know that song that you just played
    From when I was at sea.
Adrift, a voice would rise and fade
    With that same melody.

Her words would lap against my boat
    From somewhere down below.
Every dripping, splashing note
    Was tempting me to go.

Some nights I'd hear her song and stare
    Into the endless deep
And wake in panic, unaware
    Of swimming in my sleep.

I hadn't heard it played since then—
    I've been so long ashore.
I almost felt her grip again,
    Tugging at my oar.

I'll get some slats to mend the walls.
　I'll fix the roof to where at least
　It only leaks when hard rain falls.
I'll bar the door to man or beast.

　I'll put a table where the sun
　Or moon can give me light to see
The lines I've penned or left undone
Or learn the books I've brought with me.

I'll have a cot where I can sleep.
　I'll fix a corner made for prayer:
A print of Christ shepherding sheep
　Nailed up beside a wooden chair.

Some nights I'll lie out in the grass.
I'll shrink to dust beneath the sky.
The geese will tell me, when they pass,
　When it's close to time to die.

Did you lose your leaves again?
I swear last time I checked
Every single twig you have
Was gorgeously bedecked.

Now look at your empty bough,
Your canopy is wrecked!
Oh! But what a detailed frame—
Who was your architect?

All summer long I worked at growing,
Holding up my flowers for showing
And now look what you've done!

You've come out with those shears again
Gutting where my growth had been:
I'm back where I'd begun.

If this is how it's going to be
Why did you plant and water me
And give me all that sun?

You tell me that it's for my good
Then stack me up for kindling wood.

Sometimes I think I hear the front door shut,
Most often late at night when sleep has fled
And left me lying wide awake upset
With worry wondering have you seen God yet
Or was there pain or what words—last—were said
Or some such something gnawing at my gut.

I think I hear the click and next expect
To hear your footsteps coming down the hall
Or water filling up the bathroom sink.
All this before my mind has time to think:
There is no way it could be you at all.
Besides, I locked the door and double-checked.

Sometimes I call out, even so, to you:
Get the light—hang the towel when you're through!

She works all night to fabricate
Her web, again, between the gate
And fence post—threaded constellate—
Then sits in high-strung, anxious wait
Until an insect finds its fate
And makes the network undulate
In frantic fight like fish on bait.

What happens next, I hesitate:
That part of nature that I hate.

I miss those nights from childhood when I ran
Breathless through abandoned, moonlit streets
But seconds freed from blankets, covers, sheets—
Awakened when the engine first began
To blare its horn beyond the edge of town.
The rolling rumble rattled miles of track
Before its lone light broke into the black
And slowed its pace for me to chase it down
And climb aboard the last car as it crept
Off into the dark along the rail.
I would sit and watch the town lights pale
Until my eyes grew heavy and I slept.

How many hours I've scratched at dirt
Or picked off pieces from dried leaves
Or traced your name out on my skirt
Or scolded God through handkerchiefs
Or told you what I did that day
Or read from poems you would read
Or prayed from prayers that you would pray
Or cleared the grave of worm and weed
Or pressed my forehead to my hand
Or wished that I could understand.

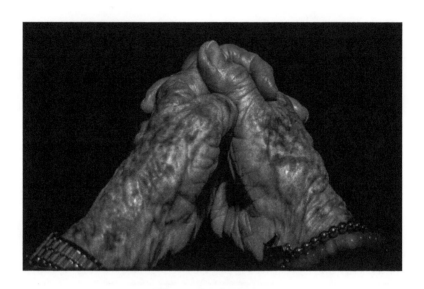

Were I offered either or,
I'd yield a vault of gold
Or summers on a sea swept shore,
Or stars a millionfold.
I'd wave the rights to any throne
And toss away the key
To any fortress—strong of stone—
If it were granted me.
No riches numbered more than sands,
Nor power over men:
Rather, let me touch her hands
Or hear her voice again.

Maybe someday, long from now—
Fair skin, hair gray, and wrinkled brow—
Your step will stop and gaze will fix
As sunset embers intermix
In wind-swept brushstrokes set aglow
That take you back years, years ago
To someday, somewhere you and I
Had stood to watch the burning sky
Blaze out across the distance, broad,
And talked of boys and dance and God.

I stood a while out at the fence
To visit with a horse.
Not a word of his made sense!
Still yet, I tried to force
A smile or chuckle when his head
Reared back in whinnied play
As if the joke of what he'd said
Was something I would say.

They tried to tell me you were gone
Last night—the clouds and rain.
They hid the moon and claimed that dawn
Would never come again.

For hours they made as if the end
Were here—and you, expired.
Such storms—the clouds and rain and wind
Did all that was required

To make me think darkness prevailed—
To make me think you dead.
But, once again, their try has failed
And you've come back instead.

No worry over finding food:
They leave it here and there,
And watch to guarantee each one
Takes no more than their share.

We have an island where we climb
The ropes and shake the trees,
With keepers noting every move
In their analyses.

Too hot or cold, we go inside
And watch the people pass.
Some stop and puff their cheeks and press
Their fingers at the glass.

There's little that we want for here.
We're safely reconciled
As captives, free to pass the days
Dreaming of the wild.

The four who chose to stick around
When I approached the gate
(The rest with disapproving sound
As one though twenty-eight
Or thirty quickly trampled ground
Far-off then turned to wait)
Were kind enough to silhouette
Themselves against the glow
(Having deemed me not a threat—
No prod nor brand to show)
And pose a pasteurized quartet—
One shot, then grunt and go.

When my time comes to walk the pier
(That is to say when death is near)
I hope the powers that be permit
A little time for me to sit
And test the water with my toes
Before I gasp and plug my nose
And sink into the dark unknown
Instead of being dragged and thrown.

And then the house lights dimmed to dark
And I walked out to center stage
Knowing this, at my late age,
Would have to be my last remark.

I spoke my gratitude to God.
I sighed to utter my last word.
Then from some distant place I heard
A single pair of hands applaud.

I know it's late
And we should go
But if we wait
The afterglow
Will captivate
In stunning show
And compensate
For debts we owe.

Printed in the USA
CPSIA information can be obtained
at www.ICGtesting.com
LVHW052004010923
756988LV00022B/96